HOORAY! HOORAY!

NOWRUZ

IS

HERE!

Written & Illustrated by

Mojgan
Roohani

HOORAY! NEW YEAR SPRINGTIME IS HERE!

Growing Sabzeh!
First day
soak seeds in Water for a day

Growing Sabzeh!
Second day
Drain water. Wrap seeds in a soft moist towel for a day

Growing Sabzeh!
Third day
Unwrap seeds. Put seeds in dish. Cover them with a small moist towel for a day.

Growing Sabzeh!
Don't Forget!
Remove towel after Third day. For two weeks, sprinkle Sabzeh with water everyday. Keep them outdoors to grow.

To do list countdown   Nowruz

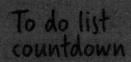

10. Prepare Sabzeh
9. New plants for garden
8. Spring-clean house
7. Shop for new clothes
6. To market for goldfish
5. Decorate eggs
4. Prepare Haft Sîn
3. Bonfire for Chaharshanbeh Suri
2. Cook Sabzi Polo Mahi
1. Nowruz party and begin thirteen days of fun!

Don't forget!
There is a game at the end

First published 2018 by CreateSpace for Amazon
www.amazon.com
ISBN -978-1986767163

Copyright ©Mojgan Roohani 2018
The right of Mojgan Roohani to be identified as the author and the illustrator of this work has been asserted.

To all my friends who have taken the time for a detailed look
at my book and share their thoughts, my truly grateful thanks!

A special thanks comes from my heart to Dr. Latifeh Hagigi
for her attention to the transliteration of the Persian words.

Lastly how can I thank my long-time encourager, collaborator,
editor, and above all very dear friend Viva Tomlin? Take a look
at the end of the book for more about the journey we have
had together as writers and creators of books!

For my dear husband, Iraj,
and Mahtab, Mateen and Melody,
and for all children everywhere.

I love when soon it will be Nowruz!
Nowruz means New Year!

It has been celebrated from long long ago,
at the beginning of spring.

Today, each country has its own customs.
But in my family we keep some of
the old Persian traditions.

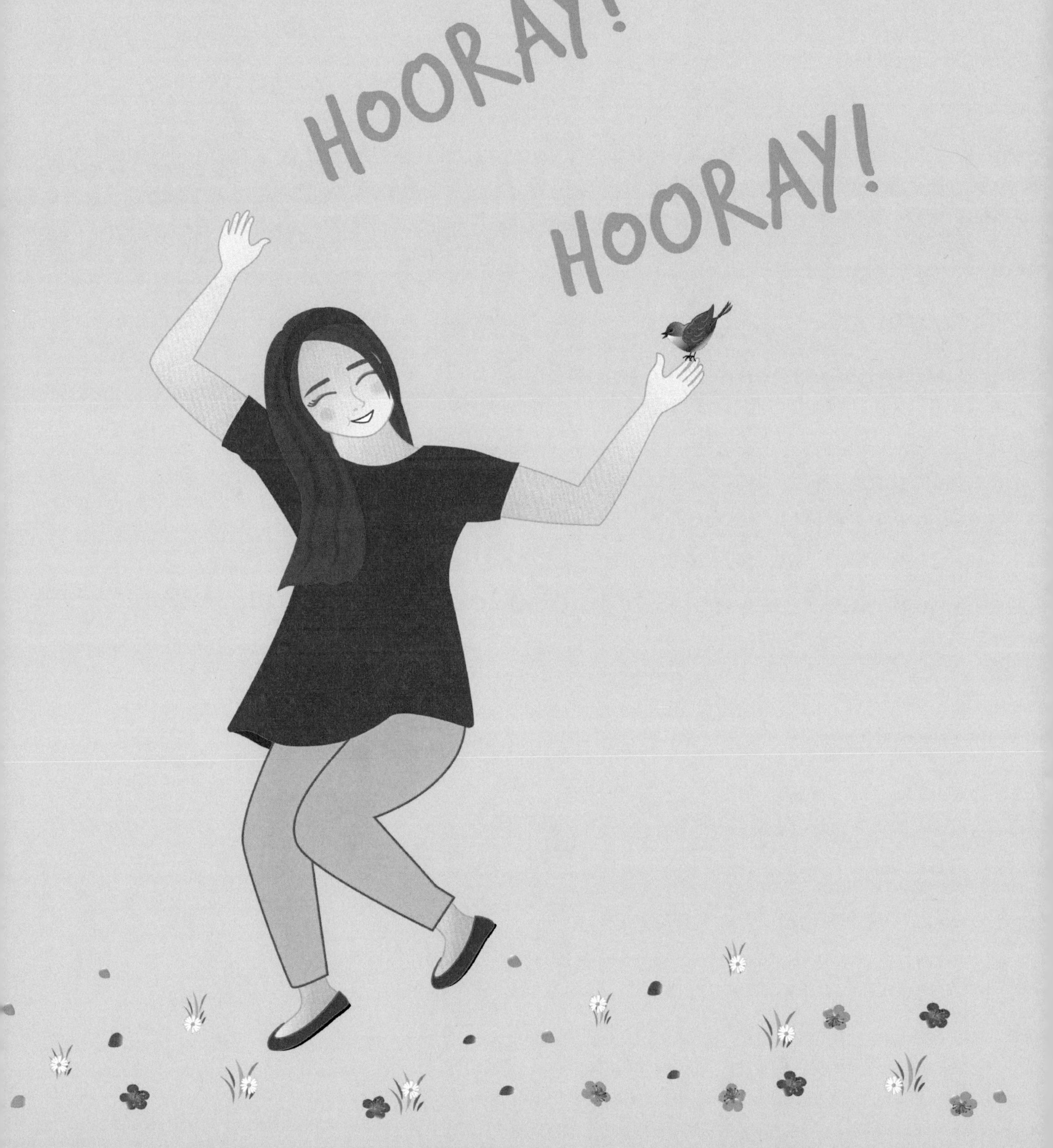
HOORAY!
HOORAY!

I love that my Grandma teaches me how
to grow the beautiful dishes of green shoots
for Nowruz.

We like to use wheat seeds or lentils.
My job is to water the seeds.

I get so excited everyday when I see
the shoots growing little by little.
After two weeks they are tall and green!
They show our hope for good food all year long.
We call it Sabzeh.

SABZEH!

Growing Sabzeh shows
that our Nowruz preparations have begun!

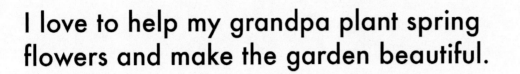

I love to help my grandpa plant spring flowers and make the garden beautiful.

Our cherry tree is covered with blossoms. The beauty of the garden reminds us that winter has passed and the spring has come.

We call this Bahar Amad.

BAHAR AMAD

I love how we make our home
sparkling clean for Nowruz!

My brother, sister and I
all help the family
with spring-cleaning.

We call this Khuneh takuni.

KHUNEH
TAKUNI

It means shaking the dust
out of the house!

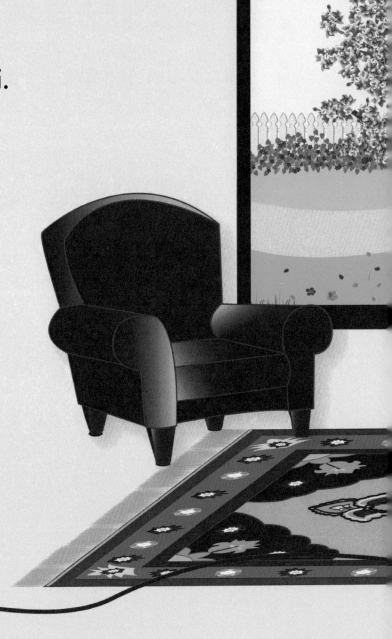

I love this Nowruz tradition!
Our parents take us shopping.
We start the New Year with
new shoes and new clothes!

We call this Lebas-e Now.

LEBAS-E
NOW

I love to go to the Persian market before Nowruz.

There are special Nowruz sweets, fruits, and nuts that we buy for our Nowruz table.

Some other special items that go on the table are spices, hyacinths and goldfish.

My sister wants a pink hyacinth but she can't find one. So she picks a blue one.

My brother and I choose the best Nowruz goldfish.

We call this Nowruz goldfish Mahi Ghermez-e Eyd.

MAHI GHERMEZ-E EYD

I love when my mom and I decorate eggs
for our Nowruz table.

They show the cycle of new life.

We paint them with joyful colors
and add pretty designs!

We call this Tokhm-e Morgh-e Rangi.

TOKHM-E
MORGH-E
RANGI

I love when my mom takes out
our beautiful table cloth for Nowruz.

It is fun to decorate the Nowruz table!
We choose seven things beginning with
the Persian letter 'Sîn' which is 's',
to put on our tablecloth.

Serkeh
(Vinegar)

We call it Sofreh-ye Haft Sîn.

Senjed
(Persian
Wild Olive)

SOFREH-YE HAFT SÎN

Somagh
(Sumac)

Sîb
(Apple)

We also put other things
on our Haft Sîn table
that have a special meaning
in our history, such as
colored eggs, sweet pastries,
a candle, a mirror, a Holy book
or a book of poetry and rose water
in a small pitcher.

Sabzeh
(Green Shoots)

Sekeh
(Coin)

Sir
(Garlic)

Samanu
(Wheat Germ
Pudding)

Sonbol
(Hyacinth)

In the old days people
said these things would bring
health, prosperity and joy.

I love the Eve before the last Wednesday before Nowruz. We get together around small bonfires and jump over the flames. While we jump over the fire, we sing a very old song:

Zardi-ye man az to
Sorkhi-ye to az man

Fire take all our sickness away!
Fire give us your health and wealth!

My grandma tells how neighbors used to come to the door on this night covered with a long veil to hide who they were. They banged on pots with spoons and asked for nuts, sweets or candies.

This night is called
Chaharshanbeh Suri.

CHAHARSHANBEH
SURI

I love when I see my dad come home with a big white fish from the market.

We all help to prepare a dish of rice mixed with green herbs to serve with the white fish.

This is a special and tasty dish we eat on the first day of Nowruz!

We call this Sabzi Polo Mahi.

SABZI POLO MAHI

I love when Nowruz is almost here!
At last it is time to get ready and put on
our new clothes.

I can't wait for my grandparents, aunts,
uncles, cousins and our friends to arrive!
With my sister and my brother we
welcome everyone.

My sister is so happy! Our cousin
has brought her the pink hyacinth.

We wait for the moment of the
New Year. We call this moment,
when the spring Equinox comes,
Sãl Tahvil.

SÃL TAHVIL

We gather around the table
to count down together!

10 9 8 7 6 5 4 3 2 1

Hooray! Hooray! Nowruz is here!
We greet this day with joy
and gladness.
We hug and say, "Happy Nowruz!"
"Eyd-e Shoma Mobarak!"

EYD-E SHOMA MOBARAK

I love the celebration of Nowruz!

We dance, sing, and eat together.

Later, our Grandma and Grandpa give us
money as a gift for Nowruz!
They do this to bring us more good fortune.

We call this Eydi.

EYDI

I love the last day of Nowruz!
After twelve days of visiting
relatives and friends,
then comes the thirteenth day.
Our celebrations come to an end.

It is the last day of Nowruz!
We go to the countryside,
or to a park, for picnics
and to enjoy being in nature.

This is called Sizdah Bedar.

SIZDAH BEDAR

Some people tie grass together
on this day for good luck all year.

Every day of Nowruz has been
very joyful!

HAPPY NEW YEAR!
HAPPY NOWRUZ!

Candle

Sonbol
(Hyacinth)

Samanu
(Wheat Germ
Pudding)

Mirror

Sekkeh
(Coin)

Goldfish

Mix Nuts

**Persian
Sweets**

Somagh
(Sumac)

Rose Water

Holy Book

Serkeh
(Vinegar)

Senjed
(Oleaster)

Decorated Eggs

Sabzeh
(Green Shoot)

Sīb
(Apple)

Sīr
(Garlic)

NOWRUZ GAME

* Look in the book
to find
these activities
and their Persian names.
* Then draw a line from
each picture
to the Persian title.

SABZEH

♦♦♦♦♦

TOKHM-E MORGH-E RANGI

♦♦♦♦♦

KHUNEH TAKUNI

♦♦♦♦♦

SOFREH-YE HAFT SÎN

♦♦♦♦♦

SABZI POLO MAHI

♦♦♦♦♦

LEBAS-E NOW

♦♦♦♦♦

MAHI GHERMEZ-E EYD

♦♦♦♦♦

SIZDAH BEDAR

♦♦♦♦♦

EYDI

♦♦♦♦♦

CHAHARSHANBEH SURI

A little about me:

I am a graphic designer whose
passion for children's books has gradually
taken me deeper and deeper into the realms of
storytelling and book illustration. I live in Santa Monica,
CA, with my husband and children who share my other passion,
our magical garden with a fountain, fruit trees, desert flowering
bushes and lots of roses.

The idea for this book has been in my mind for many years and
has evolved from Nowruz to Nowruz as my children grew up and
passed from preschool to kindergarten to elementary school and
beyond! They and their teachers always wanted something cultural
and colorful to share in the classroom along with one of the activities
such as decorating eggs or preparing to grow a dish of green shoots!
So I feel great joy that I finally have completed this labor of love!

Teamwork is a wonderful gift! My friend Viva and I are a special team!
Together we have learned and developed the many skills needed for
book production, for many years. Late into the night over endless
coffees, we have shared the agonizing times, but mostly built
joyful memories as we learned in our different fields to develop
our own storytelling voice, the art of design, formatting,
writing and publishing for our professional careers,
celebrating as seemingly insurmountable mountains
were scaled, to reach a point
where our creative dreams
could become realized.

Made in the USA
San Bernardino, CA
11 March 2019